Pure Worship

Dora Mar

Dora Mar Books
www.doramarbooks.com

Pure Worship

Copyright © 2010 by Dora Mar. All rights reserved.

Published 2010 by Dora Mar Books

www.doramarbooks.com

Scripture quotations are taken from the Holy Bible, *KJV – King James Version*. Authorized King James Version.

Cover design and photos by Robert Gromadzki

First Edition, 2010

Printed in the United States of America

ISBN 978-0-578-07983-7

Dedication

This book is dedicated to God the Father, The Son, and The Holy Spirit...

My family, friends, pets and those that have gone before me...

I would like to thank Robert for his unconditional support, editing assistance, and extending his creative talents graciously for this assignment.

Contents

The Heart of the Father 10

The Blood of the Lamb 16

The Voice of The Holy Spirit 24

Purity In Love 32

Worship in Spirit and Truth 36

Warfare 40

Preface

Within these pages is a powerful message to understand the heart of the Father and an admonishment to serve our Lord in a way that is pleasing to Him.

"No one can come to the Father, except by me"... these are the words of Christ.

You cannot come to the Father without a pure heart.

"Blessed are the pure in heart: for they shall see God."
(Matthew 5:8)

You must first: repent, receive His precious Son's sacrificial death and resurrection for atonement of your sins, receive His Holy Spirit; then you may enter into the Father's courts with thanksgiving and praise!

"And he said unto them, These are the words which I spake unto you, while I was yet with you, that all things must be fulfilled, which were written in the law of Moses, and in the prophets, and in the psalms, concerning me.

Then opened he their understanding, that they might understand the scriptures, And said unto them, Thus it is written, and thus it behooved Christ to suffer, and to rise from the dead the third day: And that repentance and remission of sins should be preached in his name among all nations, beginning at Jerusalem."
(Luke 24:44-47)

We owe Christ all Honor and Glory for this sacrificial act. He paid the atonement of our sins.

"But God commendeth his love toward us, in that, while we were yet sinners, Christ died for us."
(Romans 5:8)

His Mercy and Grace is beyond our human comprehension.

In these critical days, the Father has given us a way of escape. This escape is provided by His only begotten Son, Yeshua, the Christ; through the shedding of His precious blood on Calvary Hill.

Deception has swept across the earth; false prophets have risen to excessive levels. Earthquakes, famines, floods, severe storms, volcanic eruptions are a mere example of the utter destruction that lies ahead.

"Those that have ears, hear the warnings, those that have eyes to see, see the signs, and those that have a heart that is pure, love the Lord your God; Trust in the Lord your God with thine heart and lean not onto thine own understanding."

(Proverbs 3:5)

Chapter One

The Heart of the Father

Chapter One:
The Heart of the Father

To know the heart of the Father, is to know pure worship. Who can know the Father? Only those that have a pure heart before Him. Those that have a pure heart have capitulated all of themselves unto Him. They have allowed His Holy Spirit to consume every part without exception; by receiving God's promise through His Son's redemptive blood.

The Father is the reservoir of love that pours out through His precious Son and Holy Spirit for us to receive. Those who walk in righteousness before the Lord have received His Love.

To walk in true righteousness is to walk in the righteousness of Christ. How can this be accomplished, especially when we are attacked on all sides by the enemy, which is Satan, trying to pervert our walk on every side? By living Holy - which cannot be accomplished on our own. If we seek God in everything and turn our will unto Him and allow His Holy Spirit to have reign; it is then when we will walk in the righteousness of Christ. And only then when we will know pure worship.

If we would stop listening to the balderdash around us, and listen to the pure voice of the Lord, He will speak to our heart; as it will be pure before Him.

His presence is breathtaking and beyond our comprehension. Nothing on earth could explain or know this heavenly sphere unless understood by the power of His Holy Spirit.

I have experienced pure worship, and have heard the Angels of the Lord singing around the Throne of Glory. The musical tones and voices of the angels were unlike anything I've ever heard before. The majesty was beyond human comprehension.

No one can come to the Father, lest He calls you to Him. How do you know if the Father calls you to Him? His Holy Spirit will bear witness to your calling. Those that hear His voice and turn from their wicked ways will receive His crown of Grace.

Each remnant of God has a specific call and purpose to fulfill in these days ahead. We must be surefooted and focused to receive critical instructions that must be carefully considered and heeded. If you are called to wait, you must wait. When you are called to act, you must act without hesitation or delay. It is also critical to keep your heart pure from the grievances of this world.

"Obedience is an important key that will unlock hidden treasures that God has reserved for this very hour. To obey is better than sacrifice."
(Samuel 15:22)

It was given to me that the dichotomy is the algorithm of life. But what is a dichotomy, as it applies here? A dichotomy is division of a whole into two parts; and these two parts are mutually exclusive or opposed. This means the two parts are completely separate, they cannot overlap, and one cannot be a part of the other. This applies to where we exist; as one part is worldly, and the other is of God. And quite simply an algorithm is a set of rules and instructions.

Concerning the flesh and the spirit of God; when we die to our flesh, we begin live and breathe in the Spirit of our living God (even though we still have a fleshly body).

Therefore; do not let the things of this world spoil the pure mission of the Holy Spirit at work in you. There are worldly possessions; and then there are belongings of the Spirit of God.

"Even the Spirit of truth; whom the world cannot receive, because it seeth him not, neither knoweth him: but ye know him; for he dwelleth with you, and shall be in you."
(John 14:17)

"If ye were of the world, the world would love his own: but because ye are not of the world, but I have chosen you out of the world, therefore the world hateth you."
(John 15:19)

To fulfill your purpose, you must understand the algorithm (set of instructions) of life which is the dichotomy (separation of two worlds). Separate yourself from things of this world, and surrender your flesh over to the Holy Spirit; then God will be able to use your vessel for His Glory. Then you will know the heart of the Father.

Keep in mind that our Father in Heaven is sovereign, just, loving, but also full of anger and wrath. He does not tolerate sin! AMEN.

Chapter Two

The Blood of the Lamb

Chapter Two:
The Blood of the Lamb

In our human nature we are prisoners to sin. Satan, therefore can maneuver around and through us even without our realizing this. Many today are lost to this fact, but God's word is very clear:

"Enter ye in at the strait gate: for wide is the gate, and broad is the way, that leadeth to destruction, and many there be which go in thereat:"
(Matthew 7:13)

The nature of the human flesh is to fulfill its lusts. The desire of the Holy Spirit in us is to please God. Without the Holy Spirit, we cannot please God because we are prisoners to a sinful nature.

The call to repentance is an act of obedience and faith. "But without faith it is impossible to please him: for he that cometh to God must believe that he is, and that he is a rewarder of them that diligently seek him." *(Hebrews 11:6)*

Obedience to God puts the desires of the flesh to death. In these days of perversion, convolutions, and utter disobedience to God, the results are obvious even to the unbeliever.

True repentance is realizing that you are a sinner, truly grieving over your sinful nature, accepting the Blood of Christ as sacrifice for the ultimate gift of your salvation, and completely turning from your wicked ways.

"If my people, which are called by my name, shall humble themselves, and pray, and seek my face, and turn from their wicked ways; then will I hear from heaven, and will forgive their sin, and will heal their land."

(2 Chronicles 7:14)

Without the covering of the blood of the lamb, there is no Holy protection. To be victorious in the battle that is raging in the heavenlies, and has now spilled excessively onto the earth, we must be covered with the blood of Christ. We must be prepared for this battle and arm ourselves accordingly.

"Put on the whole armour of God, that ye may be able to stand against the wiles of the devil. For we wrestle not against flesh and blood, but against principalities, against powers, against the rulers of the darkness of this world, against spiritual wickedness in high places. Wherefore take unto you the whole armour of God, that ye may be able to withstand in the evil day, and having done all, to stand. Stand therefore, having your loins girt about with truth, and having on the breastplate of righteousness; And your feet shod with the preparation of the gospel of peace; Above all, taking the shield of faith, wherewith ye shall be able to quench all the fiery darts of the wicked. And take the helmet of salvation, and the sword of the Spirit, which is the word of God:"

(Ephesians 6:11-18)

The root of the indignant spirit is trying to take root and destroy families and relationships. It is a slow, non-gaseous poison that is creeping in households quietly and effectively from the back door. This deadly root from our adversary causes individuals to have an ungrateful attitude, with a sense of entitlement to deserving self-gratification and justified self-pleasing actions. It will also cause individuals to indulge in self-pity through a recklessly resentful attitude that life has "dealt them a bad hand".

False pride is also another destructive force if left untreated will escalate in time to cause utter destruction within one's self.

"When pride cometh, then cometh shame: but with the lowly is wisdom."
(Proverbs 11:2)

"Pride goeth before destruction, and an haughty spirit before a fall."
(Proverbs 16:18)

Today, insolence is running rapid amongst the young and old. Reverence toward God has been replaced by greed, lust of the flesh, and self-fulfilling pride. Just take a look around you. Just take a step back for a moment, check yourself; what are you watching on the television and what are you allowing your children to watch and listen to? What are you filling your vessel with? Keeping in mind this it was intended by God to be a vessel of honor for His glorification. Carefully examine yourself and your household.

The flesh has many needs and desires. In order to be able to fulfill God's desire for you, you must trust Him unconditionally. This is an incredible feat; one that takes perseverance, dedication and above all, undying faith.

Right now is a great time to renew your faith. Pause now, and ask our Heavenly Father to strengthen your faith and deliver you from all unrighteousness.

May you and your house be cleansed by the Blood of the Lamb.
AMEN

"But in a great house there are not only vessels of gold and of silver, but also of wood and of earth; and some to honour, and some to dishonour. If a man therefore purge himself from these, he shall be a vessel unto honour, sanctified, and meet for the master's use, and prepared unto every good work. Flee also youthful lusts: but follow righteousness, faith, charity, peace, with them that call on the Lord out of a pure heart."

(2 Timothy 2:20-22)

Chapter Three

The Voice of The Holy Spirit

Chapter Three:
The Voice of The Holy Spirit

How do you know if it is the voice of The Holy Spirit speaking to you? The answer is purely simple.

"My sheep hear my voice, and I know them, and they follow me: And I give unto them eternal life; and they shall never perish, neither shall any man pluck them out of my hand."
(John 10:27-28)

The voice of the Holy Spirit can be gentle as a lamb and mighty as a roaring lion. With discernment, you will be able to hear the voice of comfort, instruction and correction.

There is much chatter all around. The unholy chatter around you is trying to disorient, confuse and cloud your right judgment. It is no wonder that today there is a rising fascination with demons, zombies, vampires, werewolves, ghosts and many other perverting evil spirits. This causes people to enter into a catatonic state; unable to fully hear the Holy Spirit. Controlled by evil spirits unknowingly!

Take time right now and ask our Heavenly Father if there is a cloud of confusion blocking your reception; and to remove it and allow you to see the areas where you require deliverance!

May the Lord bless you and open your eyes to see clearly the areas that need His healing and Divine touch!

Sometimes, we will hear from the Holy Spirit in the most unexpected times and places. Many years ago I was called to take a friend home from the hospital that was treated for a broken collar bone... When I arrived at the hospital, my friend had another friend that arrived before me and decided to have them take him home. As I turned to leave the reception area of the hospital, I felt compelled to call home on the payphone and let them know that I would be coming home sooner than I had anticipated. I was told that an old friend that we had not seen in years came by to notify us that another friend (that we had not seen in a while) was in the same hospital and was expected to die that evening. I sighed and paused for a moment and said a silent prayer for him and turned to exit the hospital. Just then, as if involuntarily, I turned around headed toward the reception desk and said "you have a Jeff in intensive care, and I need to see him". The receptionist looked up at me reluctantly and said "do you know his last name? And I replied" no, but if you will let me use your phone I can find out". She agreed, and fortunately our other friend was still at my home and was able to give me Jeff's last name. The receptionist then said to me "Well obviously you are not a family member". I said that he had worked for my uncle on some odd jobs and I would feed him lunch on occasion. I also added, "His friend told us that he is expected to die by evening, so what would it hurt if I went up there to pray over him".

She agreed to call up to the intensive care unit and ask the head nurse if this would be ok. She then told me I could go up to the intensive care unit and meet the head nurse at the door.

I proceeded up to meet the head nurse and explained to her that I was a friend of Jeff's and that I was aware that he would not make it through the night. She confirmed this and told me he was in a coma with an extremely deadly fever and hooked up to many machines. We then walked into the room together; she said she had to accompany me due to the nature of his condition.

As I looked at Jeff lying there on a rotating bed with all sorts of tubes connected to him, I was taken aback. The nurse asked me if I was ok and if I still could handle looking at him in this condition. Just then

I felt compelled by the Holy Spirit to place my hand on the edge of the bed, and I began to pray. I started out in English and then the Holy Spirit took over and I was praying in God's heavenly language very quietly as the nurse waited for me by the door. The nurse gave me her name and told me that I could call her in the morning and she would let me know what time he had passed away. She reiterated to me that no one in his condition has ever survived. When I finished, I thanked the nurse and left the hospital.

The next morning, instead of calling, I returned to the hospital to see if I could meet with that nurse so she could give me the details of his situation. I proceeded to head directly up to the intensive care unit and opened the door and peeked in to see if I could see the nurse from the night before. As I opened the door and looked in, I saw another nurse look at me and then motion to me to wait. She looked at me with fright so I became concerned as I waited outside the ICU door. Just then I heard over the loud speaker a certain "code" was being broadcast several times in row. Within what seemed like moments, two hospital security guards came up to me and asked me if I was the girl that prayed for a man last night. I answered, "Yes, I prayed for him and the nurse witnessed". At this point I thought they were going to accuse me of pulling the plug. They said that they were called to keep me waiting until the Doctor arrived. I asked them "what does he want with me". They said that all they knew was that they had to wait with me until the Doctor arrived to talk with me.

The Doctor arrived within minutes. The first thing he said to me was, "Are you a witch?" I did not appreciate this question and became very angry. He then said "I want to know what power you used to heal this man that was not supposed to live through the night?" The nurse reported to him that after I left last night, Jeff's fever broke and he came out of the coma. I told him I was just an instrument of the Lord and that Yeshua healed him! The Doctor then said to me that he did not believe in miracles but he had to admit this definitely was one! I then said, "let me in to see him!". As I entered his room, Jeff became very excited, although he could not speak due to a tracheal tube that was still attached. Keep in mind he did not know me very well at this time, he had only seen me a few times when he worked for my uncle, when I would give him lunch on occasion. He sat up and motioned me to come closer. He then motioned for me to give him a pen and paper. He wrote, "are you an Angel?' I answered that I was sent by God to pray for him and asked if he remembered me. He wrote back, yes and that he had something to tell me.

In short, this is what he told me....when he was in the coma; he saw light shining from behind him and heard the voice of God. Then he saw me in the room touching the edge of the bed and praying in a language that he did not understand. He asked God, "who is she, she looks familiar?" God answered by telling him that I was His very own that was called to pray for him, and the language was His heavenly language, and that I was praying on his behalf. After some time of visiting him every day in the hospital, he accepted Christ as his Savior that fateful day and so much more transpired through this miraculous event. Jeff has since brought his friend to Christ before his passing away from throat cancer. This was the very same friend that was over our home telling of Jeff's traumatic event many years ago. He also found out that the doctor that treated him during that time had received Christ as his Savior due to this miracle. Jeff was known throughout the hospital as, "the miracle man". I am sure countless others in need of salvation were brought to the Lord by this one precious man; whom God loved so much that he sent me to pray for him in such an inconceivable way.

Brace yourselves and be covered by the precious Blood of the Lamb of God! AMEN.

Chapter Four

Purity In Love

Chapter Four:
Purity In Love

Purity in Love, I will praise your Holy Name

I lay my burdens unto thee,
For your grace and mercy covers me...

Purity in Love, I will praise your Holy Name

Holy Spirit Fall a fresh on me,
ignite your Holy Fire in me....

Purity in Love, I will praise you Holy Name

Father, Son and Holy Spirit...
Three as one, I sing unto thee...

Purity in Love, I will praise your Holy Name

Just as the appointed Priest could not enter into the Holy of Holies within the Tabernacle of God in days of old; without being cleansed by the blood of the lamb which represented Christ, we also cannot enter. We simply cannot barge in on the Father and demand our request be honored. He is Holy, a just Father, and an omnipotent God!

After being sanctified by the blood of Christ, we may enter His gates with thanksgiving and praise. It is then you will experience the Purity in Love of our Heavenly Father which penetrates to the depths of our souls. You will be consumed by His Holy Fire which is so magnificent and beyond comprehension. Only then can you experience a freedom that liberates your flesh in order to receive all that Our Father desires you to be in your position as you sojourn here on earth.

Those that He has entrusted the keys to His kingdom, have a great responsibility. To be able to fulfill the requirements, The Holy Spirit has to guide and direct you in EVERY situation.

May you experience Pure Worship before the Lord on High!
AMEN.

Chapter Five

Worship in Spirit and Truth

Chapter Five:
Worship in Spirit and Truth

Each of Gods's chosen ones have been given specific gifts. These gifts are revealed to us by His Holy Spirit.

"Now there are diversities of gifts, but the same Spirit. And there are differences of administrations, but the same Lord. And there are diversities of operations, but it is the same God which worketh all in all. But the manifestation of the Spirit is given to every man to profit withal. For to one is given by the Spirit the word of wisdom; to another the word of knowledge by the same Spirit; To another faith by the same Spirit; to another the gifts of healing by the same Spirit; To another the working of miracles; to another prophecy; to another discerning of spirits; to another divers kinds of tongues; to another the interpretation of tongues: But all these worketh that one and the selfsame Spirit, dividing to every man severally as he will. For as the body is one, and hath many members, and all the members of that one body, being many, are one body: so also is Christ. For by one Spirit are we all baptized into one body, whether we be Jews or

Gentiles, whether we be bond or free; and have been all made to drink into one Spirit." *(1 Corinthians 12:4-13)*

It is our responsibility to use these precious gifts carefully and in accordance with God's divine plan for each of us. How do you know what gift you have been given? Seek Him earnestly and without reproach, he will reveal your gift according to the measure in which you were given. If your intensions are pure, He will reveal new insights to you that you never dreamed possible regarding your gifting and position here on earth.

If you have been given the gift of speaking in tongues, guard this gift with a pure heart. There are counterfeit, demonic tongues that cause my spirit to shutter when I hear them. Again, you will know this by the power of the Holy Spirit working in you.

Fasting and praying is essential; according to the leading of the Holy Spirit in this area. For when you pray in the Holy Spirit, the enemy cannot know what you are praying. Miraculous events will occur.

May our God of Peace grant you power by His Holy Spirit to discern hidden truths that are waiting to be revealed in these days ahead. AMEN!

Chapter Six

Warfare

Chapter Six:
Warfare

Daring to be a mighty warrior for God is not always a highly regarded position by men. Although this is true, we must strive to please God, not man.

"Hast thou not known? hast thou not heard, that the everlasting God, the LORD, the Creator of the ends of the earth, fainteth not, neither is weary? there is no searching of his understanding. He giveth power to the faint; and to them that have no might he increaseth strength. Even the youths shall faint and be weary, and the young men shall utterly fall: But they that wait upon the LORD shall renew their strength; they shall mount up with wings as eagles; they shall run, and not be weary; and they shall walk, and not faint."
(Isaiah 40:28-31)

Several months ago I had a dream. I dreamt of turbulent waters all around and as far as I could see. I, along with several others, was in these turbulent waters. The waves were crashing all around us, but we in the waters were all at peace and staying afloat without any (visible) life saving provisions. Then there were those in rafts floating all around us in the waters, looking down at us with pity because they felt smug and safe in their rafts.

I asked the Lord the meaning of this dream and He told me; those who are in the turbulent waters with no apparent life saving provisions are my remnants that are being supernaturally provided for in these turbulent days. And those who think they are safe and smug in the rafts afloat in the turbulent waters, are not. They are being deceived and have a false sense of security and are not heeding the true word of God. He said they bastardize His Holy Word and His fury is raging.

God's Holy Scripture should not be taken out of context. You cannot pick and choose what Scripture will work for a fleshly agenda. This is not what God's word was intended for.

"All scripture is given by inspiration of God, and is profitable for doctrine, for reproof, for correction, for instruction in righteousness: That the man of God may be perfect, thoroughly furnished unto all good works."

(2 Timothy 3:16-17)

"Without natural affection, trucebreakers, false accusers, incontinent, fierce, despisers of those that are good, Traitors, heady, highminded, lovers of pleasures more than lovers of God; Having a form of godliness, but denying the power thereof: from such turn away."

(2 Timothy 3:3-5)

Many are being led to slaughter because their vision is blocked by a veil of deception, and the words spoken to them are pleasing to the ear; giving a false comfort for a season. But eventually, it will bring them only bitterness and confusion.

You see, our enemy, which is Satan, is at war trying to deface us before God. Effortlessly going about his business on this Earth to pervert and deceive; while using his demons as pawns to deflect us from the truth. As I mentioned in the previous chapter, we must arm ourselves daily to survive this perilous war. If we do not, we become oblivious to the destructive force that is at work to obliterate our mission here. Just as a soldier in the army must have a strategic plan of action; so must we as warriors in God's army.

"No weapon that is formed against thee shall prosper; and every tongue that shall rise against thee in judgment thou shalt condemn. This is the heritage of the servants of the LORD, and their righteousness is of me, saith the LORD."

(Isaiah 54:17)

These villains have names and their only assignment is to destroy God' people by any possible means they can. Their jealousies toward us are beyond our comprehension, even though they have chosen their own dreadful fate; they seek to devour every breath of life within us. You must be aware lest you fall for their evil tactics. This is serious and critical that we arm ourselves daily and know how to defend ourselves from this perverse enemy.

"And one of the multitude answered and said, Master, I have brought unto thee my son, which hath a dumb spirit; And wheresoever he taketh him, he teareth him: and he foameth, and gnasheth with his teeth, and pineth away: and I spake to thy disciples that they should cast him out; and they could not. He answereth him, and saith, O faithless generation, how long shall I be with you? how long shall I suffer you? bring him unto me. And they brought him unto him: and when he saw him, straightway the spirit tare him; and he fell on the ground, and wallowed foaming. And he asked his

father, How long is it ago since this came unto him? And he said, Of a child. And ofttimes it hath cast him into the fire, and into the waters, to destroy him: but if thou canst do any thing, have compassion on us, and help us. Jesus said unto him, If thou canst believe, all things are possible to him that believeth. And straightway the father of the child cried out, and said with tears, Lord, I believe; help thou mine unbelief. When Jesus saw that the people came running together, he rebuked the foul spirit, saying unto him, Thou dumb and deaf spirit, I charge thee, come out of him, and enter no more into him. And the spirit cried, and rent him sore, and came out of him: and he was as one dead; insomuch that many said, He is dead. But Jesus took him by the hand, and lifted him up; and he arose. And when he was come into the house, his disciples asked him privately, Why could not we cast him out? And he said unto them, This kind can come forth by nothing, but by prayer and fasting."
(Mark 9:17-29)

In my next book, I will be going into more detail about the names of these evil spirits and why the fight is stronger with some than others.

Evil spirits cannot have a hold on you if you do not let them. If you see an area of your life that repeatedly needs correction; an area where you lack strength to conquer, turn this area over to the Lord and allow Him to give you the strength for victory. He does not expect you to handle this alone.

Be not seduced by evil incantations that are hidden all around us. Your number one weapon against this enemy is the precious Blood of Christ our Savior! He not only shed His precious blood for our sins, He also shed His blood as a covering, a safe haven and power over the enemy which is Satan and his demons.

We should praise and glorify our Lord in every breath and fiber of our being; for His sacrificial act on our behalf.

As I mentioned earlier, there is a battle spilling over into the earth, more than ever before. There is a rise in the number of these destructive beings; causing much confusion, discord, false doctrine, and many more deceptions amongst God's people.

Making a conscious effort to resist the enemy and claim the power of Christ's blood over you and your house is an essential part in preparing for this battle.

Sometimes God will give me just one word or phrase and He desires me to search out the meaning of this. The word and phrases are always critical in discerning warnings and admonitions; just as He is guiding me through this book and the books that will follow.

"It is the glory of God to conceal a thing: but the honour of kings is to search out a matter."
(Proverbs 25:2)

He is revealing so much to His entrusted people. He is calling his people from the four corners of the earth and His will is in perfect alignment. Be blessed and encouraged, the victory is in ONE!

"I and my Father are one."
(John 10: 30)

Stand surefooted my beloved, in these critical days ahead. May you be found worthy through the Lamb of God to carry His torch of love, be of sound mind to accomplish all that He has fashioned in you. May you have the courage to stand against the wiles of the enemy, fighting with the sword of the Holy Spirit in truth and obedience. Pray without ceasing!

AMEN!

Notes

Notes

Notes

www.ingramcontent.com/pod-product-compliance
Lightning Source LLC
Chambersburg PA
CBHW051717040426
42446CB00008B/932